Contents

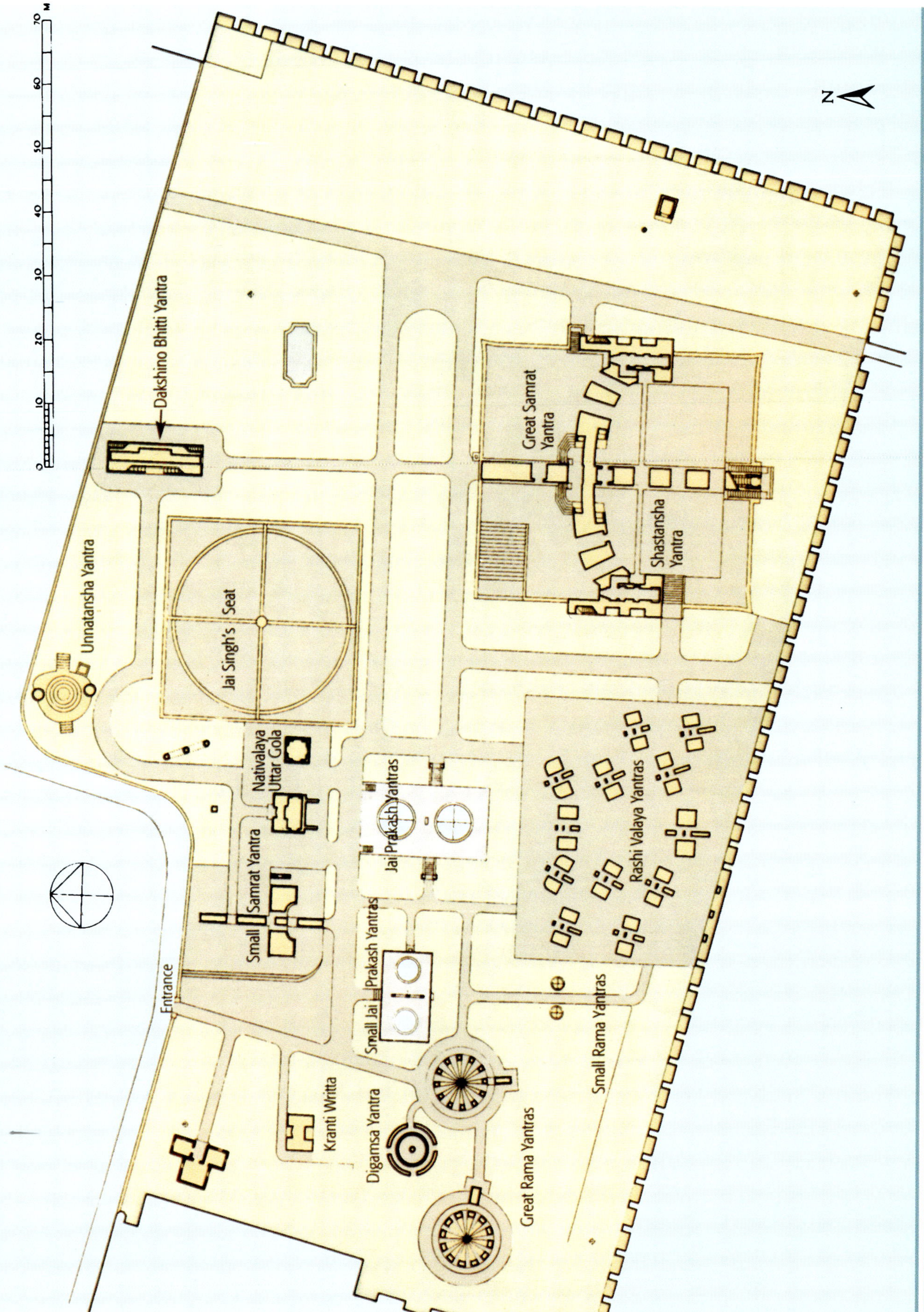

Site Plan, Observatory of Jaipur
26°55'27.4"

Introduction

The Science of Astronomy, like other sciences, was discovered in India and from India it travelled to other countries, Arabia being the first country to grasp it. The life of all creatures, vegetable or living, given birth on the face of the earth by the heavenly bodies, is composed of five Tatvas or elements, namely fire, air, water, earth, sky and their actions, auspicious or inauspicious, are governed by them which are determined by a correct measure of, time of the movements of the heavenly bodies through the twelve signs of zodiac. The latter phase is called astrology which predicts events of every thing in the world.

For purpose of observing positions of the planets above the horizon, there were perfect metal instruments in the past which have not survived to us and Maharaja Sawai Jai Singh has left a great and remarkable heritage of masonry instruments constructed at the five places, namely (1) Jaipur, (2) Delhi, (3) Ujjain, (4) Banaras and (5) Mathura, of which the largest one being at the first place. The Jaipur Astronomical Observatory is situated to the immediate south of the Jaipur City Palace and is reached by the Tripolia Gate in the Tripolia bazar, through the Chandni Chowk, and also from Sirah Deori bazar by Bandarwal and Nakkarkhana gates through Galeb chowk.

The science of Astronomy and its scion Astrology are complex sciences which cannot be understood by the general public; and besides it is not the scope of this book to impart education to the reader in their details, but the object is to give an idea of the construction and the different functions of various instruments in the observatory to the common visitor. At the same time we cannot help expressing that in order to understand the instruments one should have an elementry knowledge of Astrology.

Sawai Jai Singh II

Jai Singh was born on November 3, 1688 A.D. at Amber, the fortified capital of the Kachhawa (Kushwaha) rulers. The court astrologers had predicted to his father, Raja Bishan Singh (Vishnu Singh) of Amber, that his son would shine like Jupiter in the galaxy of princes and would prove to be the brightest star of the Kachhawa House.His visionary father made all arrangements for his early education both in martial arts and academic subjects. After the untimely death of his father in 1699 A.D., Jai Singh was coronated as the Monarch of Amber at the tender age of 11 years on January 25, 1700.

However, Maharaja continued his studies along with his princely duties as he was lucky enough to have a prudent mother, Rajmata Indra Kanwar of Kharwa near Ajmer, who made all-out efforts to see his brilliant son grow in the shadow of scholars and learned tutors. Pandit Kewal Ram of Gujarat, Pandit Ratnakar Pundarik of Maharashtra and Pandit Vidyadhar Bhattacharya of Bengal were engaged to teach him religion, philosophy, art and architecture, town planning etc. Pandit Jagannath Samrat gave him intensive coaching of the ancient Hindu treatises on astronomy and mathematics like the 'Surya Siddhanta', the master works of Aryabhatta, Varahamihira, Brahma Gupta and Bhaskaracharya - the ancient luminaries of the Hindu astronomy.

As a devoted student of astronomy, Sawai Jai Singh had universal approach to the subject and learnt in detail about the foreign classics, viz, Ptolemy's Syntaxis (Al-Magest), De La Hire's Tabulae Astronomicae, Flamsteed's Historia Coelestis Britannica, newton's Principia, Euclid's Elements, Mirza Ulugh Beg's Astronomical Tables etc.

Jai Singh was unhappy with the results he was getting from the regular brass instruments and decided to build this giant observatory to get the precision that he demanded. Before the commencement of construction he sent scholars abroad to study the foreign observatories. The emissaries returned with many manuals on astronomy containing cutting-edge technological information. One of these manuals contained a copy of La Hire's Tables. The king ordered the observatory to be built according to the details contained in the manual, while building these instruments in stone and marble he was helped by Pandit Jagannath, Kewal Ram and Vidyadhar Bhattacharya. When the construction got over, for the astonishment of the king and others, the observatory was 20 seconds more accurate than the one mentioned in Table.

The Jaipur observatory is the largest, most perfect and the best preserved observatory in the series of five made by him, which was completed by 1728 A.D.

Moghul emperor Aurangzeb was much impressed by his wit and chivalry to the

Maharaja Sawai Jai Singh II
The founder of Astronomical
Observatories.

extent of bestowing upon the young Rajput ruler the title of 'Sawai', literally one and a quarter times more than his contemporaries, which still adorns his descendant Brigadier Maharaja Sawai Bhawani Singh of Jaipur.

Sawai Jai Singh became immortal not because of the high honours received at the Moghul Court but because of the Herculian task he performed in erecting the magnanimous stone observatories.

Maharaja Sawai Jai Singh, the man with the Midas touch, who lived life king-size and created a golden era in the significant fields of art, town-planning, martial and ornamental architecture and above all, astronomy, could not celebrate the Golden Jubilee of his glorious reign. The strenuous life took its toll early and on September 21, 1743 A.D., he breathed his last at the age of 54 years. His wives', concubines and science expired with him on his Funeral Pyre at the Royal, Crematorium at Gatore.

The character and qualities of Jai Singh as narrated above are also supported by his horoscope.

Jai Singh was born under Tula Rashi (zodiac sign of Libra) which made him generous, joyous, kind hearted, lover of Art, architecture and science. The master of 4th and 5th house, Saturn is also posted in the first house under the sign of Libra. This made him an efficient administrator, a far sighted person and a super intellectual.

Jupiter in the 4th house under Capricorn and also the 10th house aspect of Saturn made him lose his father and ascend the throne at an early age. The sign scorpion in second house made him a womaniser and fond of luxurious life. It is said that he had 31 wives and the number of concubines was beyond anybody's imagination.

Horoscope of Sawai Jai Singh II Maharaja of Jaipur A.D. 1688

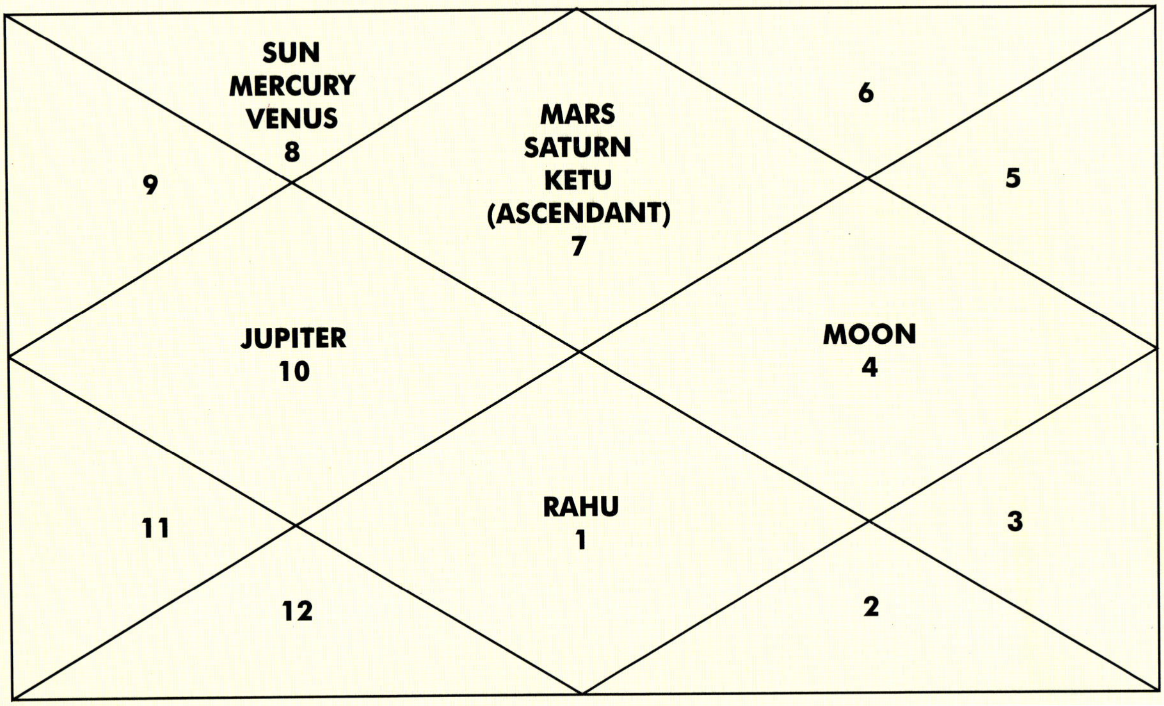

Jantar-Mantar

Jantar means "instrument", Mantar (the same word as "mantra") is usually translated "formula" but here it means "calculation". So, "Jantar Mantar" means something like "instrument for calculation". The Jantar Mantar was built in 1716 A.D. and contains 15 astronomical instrument complexes, one remains unfinished, of which 6 function with Solar lith and 11 by Lunar and Stellar reflection. These monumental instruments give a precise measure of time, of the declination of the Sun, the Azimuth, of the placement of constellations in daylight of eclipses and of another astronomical phenomena. The observatory, open to the sky is a scientific marvel and guarantees to elicit a sense of awe, even from the profane.

Although situated in the heart of the noisy city, it seems far from the madding crowd as a perfectly calm and quiet atmosphere, ideal for the contemplation of astronomical phenomena, prevails here.

The good state of preservation of the Jaipur observatory is due first of all to Chandra Dhar Sharma Guleril, who restored it in 1901. It has been well maintained from then to the present day. Now observatory is under the administrative supervision of the department of Archaeology and Museum's of the State of Rajasthan. A Superintendent and Care taker staff look after its up keep and its instruments.

At Jantar Mantar the visitor gets a glimpse of the scientific temperament of Sawai Jai Singh. The Jaipur observatory could be termed as one of the seven wonders of India and there is no exaggeration in mentioning that this post-medieval 'Stonehenge' of India, is also one of the seven wonders of the ancient astronomy in world.

Traditional Brass Instrument of Maharaja Sawai Jai Singh II

Astronomical Theories

The earth is set in the midst of an enormous hollow sphere, on the inner surface of which the stars are situated. The whole celestial sphere rotates on its axis which passes through the poles once in a day, and this accounts for the daily motion of the stars, their rising in the east, their culmination on the meridian and their final setting in the west, to rise again a few hours later in the east. The heavens are spherical. Again the Earth is situated half way between the two celestial sphere.

The Earth itself is also a sphere. Its surface must be convex in an east to west direction and it must also be convex in a north to south direction, for if we travel to the north or south the altitudes of the stars vary in accordance with this hypothesis. It is found that the variations both in the altitudes of the stars and in the times of sun rise occur regularly, hence the Earth must be regularly curved and is, therefore a sphere.

From whatever point on the Earth the stars are observed, the constellations appear of the same shape and the right ascensions, declinations and longitudes of the stars are the same. Thus a difference in the observer's position of thousands of miles makes no difference in the star's declination. This proves that a distance of several thousand miles must be the smallest fraction of the distance of the stars. Again if the Earth was largely compared with the celestial sphere, the zenith would be nearer to us than the horizon, and hence the stars would appear further apart when overhead. Also the shadow of a gnomon on the surface of the Earth tallies with that found by calculation for the centre of the Earth. Hence the dimensions of the Earth are insignificant compared with the distances of the stars.

The theory of solar system was briefly that the Earth is immovably fixed in the centre of the universe, that surrounding the Earth are the seven orbits in which the planets (Mercury, Venus, Mars, Jupiter, Saturn, Sun, and Moon) move that outside these eighth orbit or sphere containing the fixed stars, and beyond that again the ninth and last orbit of infinite dimensions that the whole heavens including all the orbits rotate daily about the Earth from east to west, and this rotation is the cause of the rising and setting of the stars.

The Hindus did not calculated angles in degrees, minutes and seconds, but they have a different system of measuring time as shown in the table below :

6 Pranas	=	one pal	=	24 minutes
60 Ghatis	=	1 day & night	=	24 hours

The whole circle is graduated into 60 Ghatis of 6 degrees each. Sidereal time is used, the time being zero when the vernal equinox

THE PLANETS

S.No.	Symbol	English	Arabic	Sanskrit	Hindi
1.	♄	Saturn	Zubal	Arki	शनि
2.	♃	Jupiter	Mushtari	Brihaspati	गुरू
3.	♂	Mars	Mirrikh	Kuja	मंगल
4.	☉	Sun	Shams	Surya	सूर्य
5.	♀	Venus	Zuhrah	Shukra	शुक्र
6.	☿	Mercury	Utarid	Budha	बुध
7.	☾	Moon	Qamar	Chandra	चन्द्र

is rising on the eastern horizon, not when the equinox is culminating on the meridian. Thus the Hindu sidereal day begins six hours earlier than the modern sidereal day. Celestial latitude and longitude are chiefly used for recording the places of the planets, as the planets are never more than five or ten degree distant from the ecliptic.

There are three systems by which the place of a heavenly body may be recorded.

1. Altitude and Azimuth
2. Declination and R.A.
3. Celestial latitude and longitude.

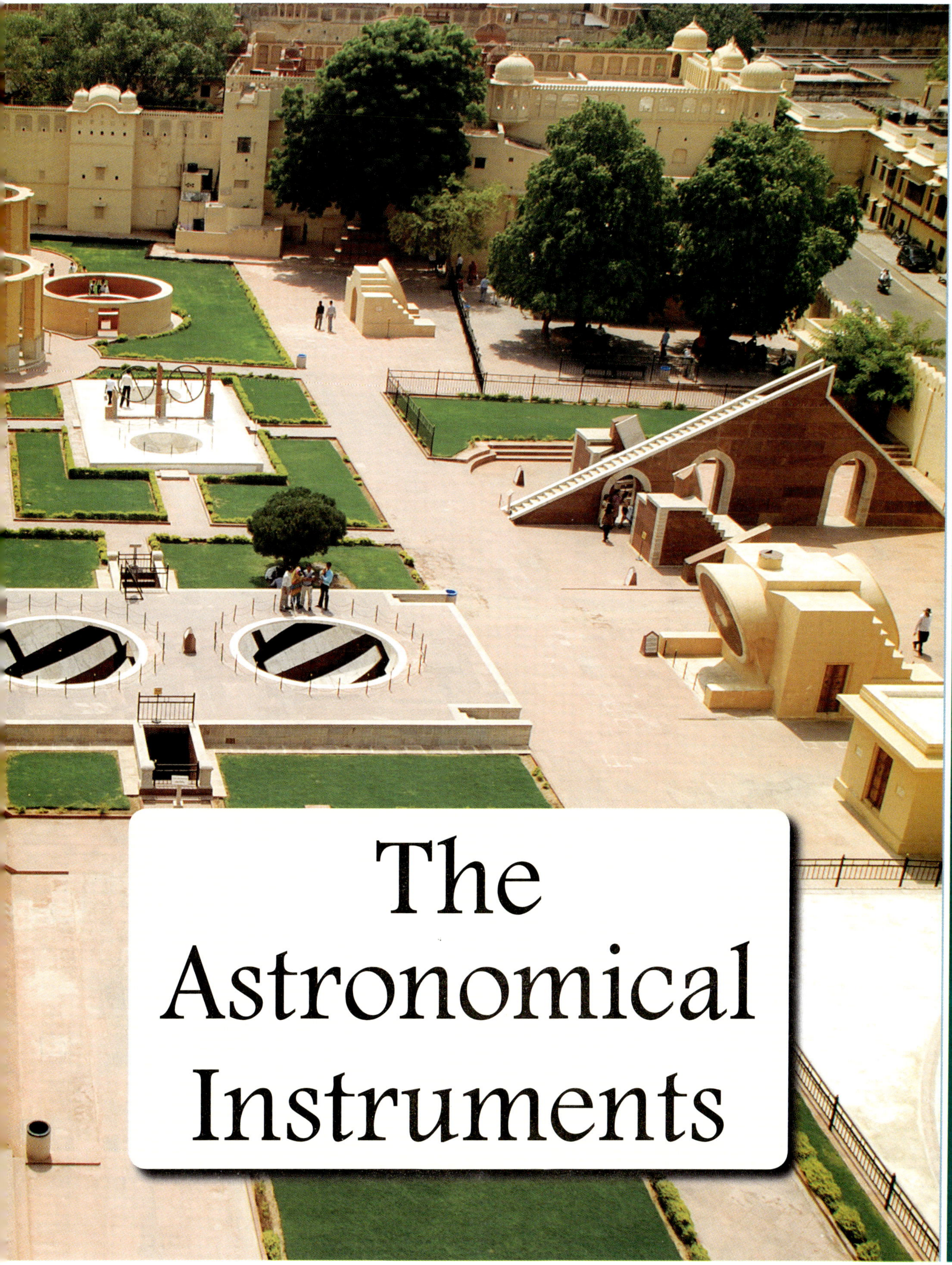

The Astronomical Instruments

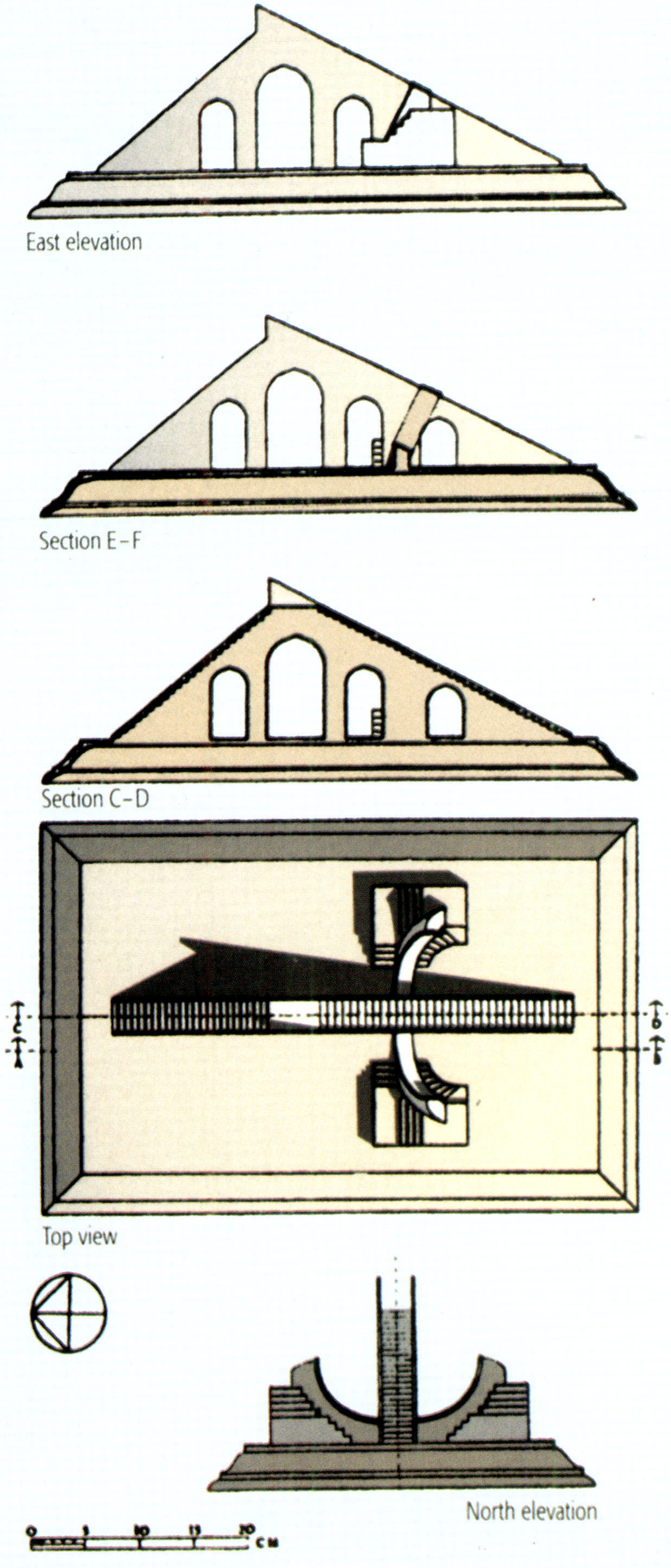

The Small Samrat Yantra.

The Small Samrat Yantra

Known as the Laghu Samrat Yantra in Hindi, this red sand-stone and white marble instrument is seen on the left, as a triangle based in the plane of local meridian and a quadrant on either side which are inclined by 27 degrees in the plane of celestial equator. The hypotenuse of the triangle makes an angle of 27 degrees, equivalent to the geographical latitude of Jaipur and is distinctly graduated in the scale of tangent used for measuring declination of heavenly bodies.

The quadrants are graduated in the time scale of hours, minutes and seconds - 6 to 12 O'clock (morning) towards west and 12 to 6 O'clock (evening) towards east. Each hour is divided by sixty minutes and each minute by three fractions, thus, making 20 seconds precision of the time observed. Each hour also stands for 15 degrees, meant for the Zenith Distance and Altitude observations.

The shadow of the hypotenuse (the gnomon) is observed on the graduated dials for reading the Local Time or the Solar Hour. The difference between the Jaipur Time and the Indian Standard Time varies from 10

TABLE OF DIFFERENCE OF THE TIME OF JAIPUR AND THE INDIAN STANDARD TIME

	5th Min.Sec.	10th Min.Sec.	15th Min.Sec.	20th Min.Sec.	25th Min.Sec.	30th Min.Sec.
January	32.10	34.18	36.13	37.50	39.9	40.8
February	40.52	41.6	41.6	40.38	39.58	39.28
March	38.26	37.15	35.52	34.15	32.55	31.6
April	29.37	28.40	26.56	25.48	28.48	24.2
May	23.28	23.44	23.5	23.15	23.37	24.21
June	25.8	25	26.48	28.12	29.16	30.18
July	31.15	32.5	32.39	33.3	33.14	33.8
August	32.46	32.8	31.17	30.12	28.15	27.10
September	23.53	23.52	22.5	20.18	18.34	16.48
October	15.18	13.54	12.39	11.38	10.56	10.28
November	10.25	10.43	11.22	12.24	13.44	15.24
December	17.20	19.18	21.48	24.18	26.39	29.44

minutes 25 seconds to 41 minutes 6 seconds which may be checked up with the Table of Time Difference. This difference of time is added to the time observed on the Equatorial Clock to find out the Indian Standard Time.

To determine the declination of the sun, a pointer is placed on the graduated hypotenuse (gnomon). Its shadow is seen intersecting the shadow of the gnomon already falling on the graduated quadrant below. This point on which the pointer is kept, indicates the declination of the sun.

The determination of accurate time is also the base of correct astrological calculations and prediction.

The most popular division of Time in antiquity as mentioned in the Surya Siddhanta, an ancient Hindu treatise on astronomy was as follows :

6 respirations (Prana)	=	1 Vikala
6 Vikalas	=	1 Danda
60 Dandas	=	1 Sidereal day

The Vishnu Purana also based on the division of Time on certain observations of bio-rhythms like 'Prana - the respiration, where ten long syllables are uttered in one 'respiration', resulting in the following Table of sub-division of time :

The following table of Time is more commonly used by the traditional astronomers and astrologers in which the time calculated for planetary positions could be incredibly as accurate as 0.2.5 seconds, i.e. two and a half fractions of a second :

1 prana	=	10 vipalas
6 pranas = 1 pala	=	60 vipalas
1 ghatika = 60 palas	=	24 minutes
2.5 ghatikas	=	1 hour
60 ghatikas	=	One day and night (Solar day)
1 pala = 60 vipalas	=	24 seconds
2.5 vipalas	=	1 second
1 vipala	=	0.2.5 seconds

Incidently, the time scale on all the quadrants and instruments was done in ghatika, palas and vipalas during the eighteenth century, which was converted to hour, minutes and seconds in 1901 A.D. at the time of restoration.

When the Sun Dials were not serviceable during the cloudy or rainy days, the Clepshydra or the Water clock replaced them.

The Dhool-Ghari was another primitive form of time measuring device.

The Great Samrat Yantra

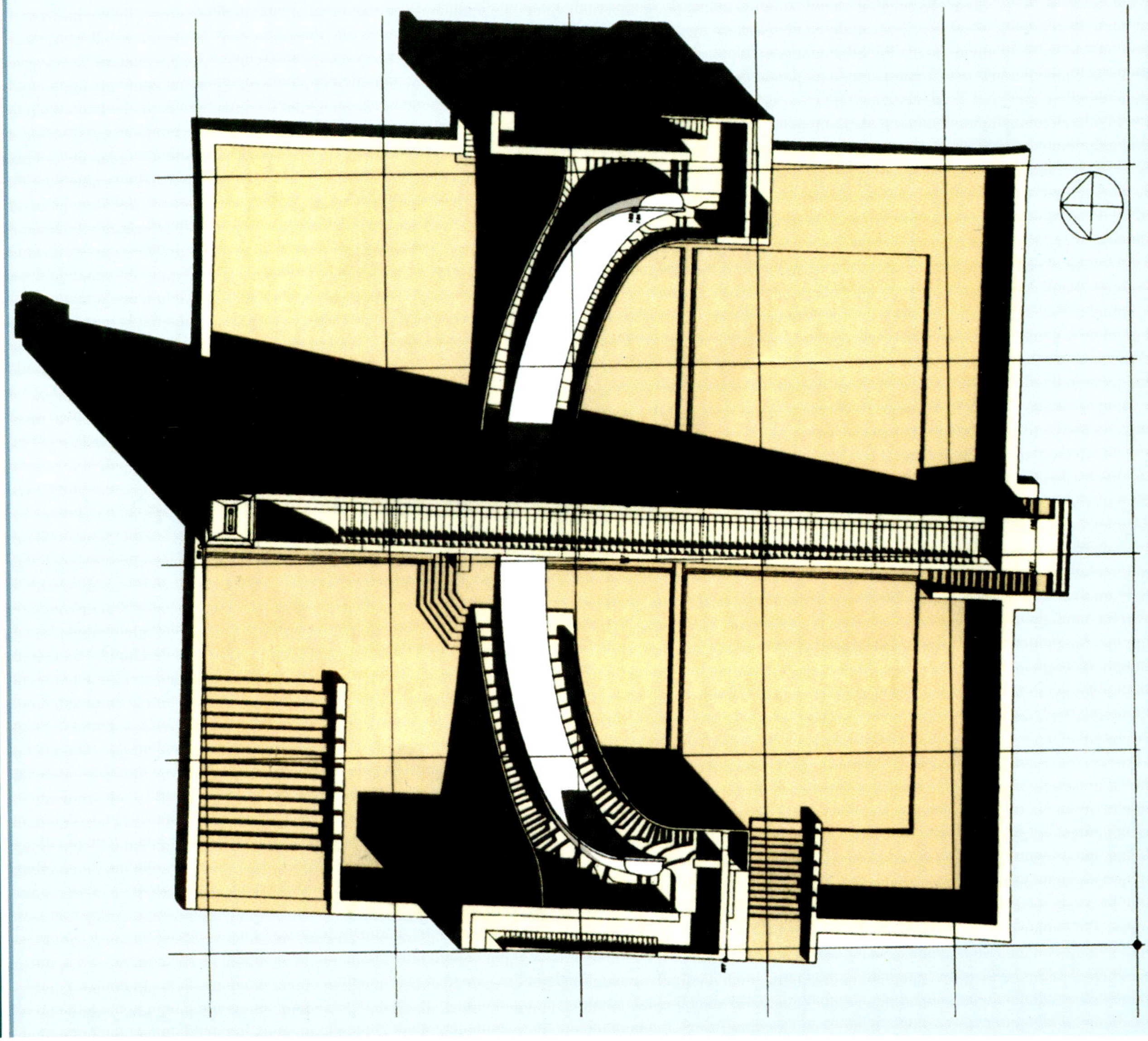

Great Samrat Yantra

It is also known as the Giant Equatorial Sun-dial. This gigantic Brihat Samrat Yantra is identical in theory and function to the Laghu Samrat Yantra, but it is five times bigger in proportions which consequently makes it ten times more precise than its smaller version. The base of this right-angled triangle is 44 metre long whereas its hypotenuse, making an angle of 27 degrees, rises to the height of 27 metres. The lofty triangle is flanked by two giant-size quadrants of 15 m radius which are graduated in hours, minutes and seconds, where the shadow of the gnomon travels about 4 metres during one hour. The same shadow moves 6 centimetres, indicating each minute which is further subdivided by thirty fractions, each standing for an incredible precision of 2 seconds.

This giant instrument helps to calculate local time, Meridian Pass time, Zenith Distance, Declination and Altitude of the heavenly bodies by the shadow of the gnomon. The calculations can also be made during night time with the help of a thread. This instrument is probably mostly used today. A number of astrologers gather here on the full moon days of June and July to study the movement and direction of the wind which helps them forecast the rains. For this purpose, a thin cloth flag is hoisted at the time of sun-set. If the flag shows easterly breeze, it is an indication of good monsoon crops. If the wind is southern in direction, the chances

of rains are scanty which can result in bad crops and famine. It is very important in the life of Indians as in India still our crops are merely dependent on monsoon. The plan of constructing and graduating the huge quadrants of the Giant Equatorial Dial is located on a large platform north-west of the Giant Equatorial Sun-Dial. The red sandstone circle of about 15 metre diameter is neatly graduated in hours, minutes and seconds, which served as the blue-print for graduating the gigantic quadrants of the Equatorial Sun-Dial later. To protect this 'blue-print' in stone, the authorities have made a metal railing all around this platform. It helped the builders, to construct the massive instrument.

The Sasthamsa Yantra

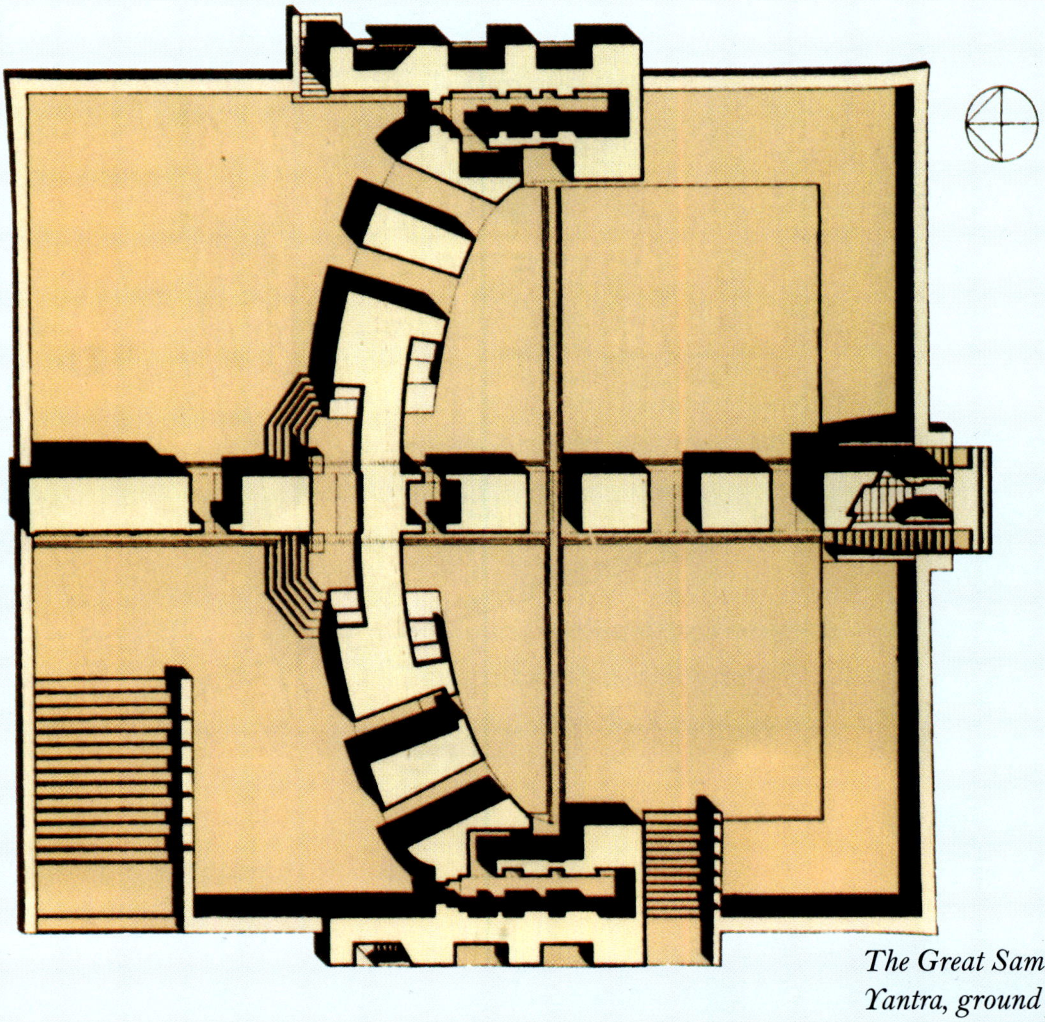

The Great Samrat Yantra, ground plan

Sasthamsa Yantra

It is nothing but a sextant which is used for finding out Zenith distance and declination. It consists of two arcs of sixty degrees each, made adjacent to the eastern and western wall of the dark room. The arcs lie north-south in the plane of local meridian. This sextant instrument is used at mid-day (Local Time) when the sun crosses the Local Meridian and its rays fall on the graduated arcs through two tiny orifices provided in the roof for the purpose.

The arcs have two scales. There are degree markings near the wall for direct observation of Declination of the Sun at noon and second scale is used for observing the Zenith Distance of the sun. At noon, the rays of the sun fall through the pin-holes made in the roof above, in the size of a tennis ball on the graduated arcs for a minute or two. With the help of the above-mentioned two scales, the Zenith Distance, Altitude, Declination etc. of the sun are directly determined at mid-day when it crosses the Local Meridian.

Palabha Yantra

It is also known as the Horizontal Sun Dial or Dhoop Ghari. It can be seen only from the top of Narivalaya. At the north south centre it has a 27 degree triangular gnomon whose shadow indicates time in "ghatis". The time observed can be verified by the hemispherical sun-dial. Such dials can still be seen on the terrace of Amber Palace, Jaisalmer Fort and elsewhere in the dwellings of astrologer-Pandits.

Dhruva-Darshak Yantra

The Dhruva-Darshak Yantra is situated eastward close to the Equatorial Sun Dial. It is also known as the Pole-star Instrument. The instrument is also made of red stone and inclined at an angle 270, the latitude of Jaipur. This is an instrument by which we can know the Geographical north, the position of pole star, ursamajor etc.

Abandoned Ecliptic Yantra

On entering the observatory, one comes across, towards right, a huge red sandstone round structure of about 3 metre diameter. The Maharaja and his team-mates realised that it would be too big a metal device to make and it would be cumbersome and impractical to rotate it on this huge base. Thus, this impressive equatorial dial was abandoned.

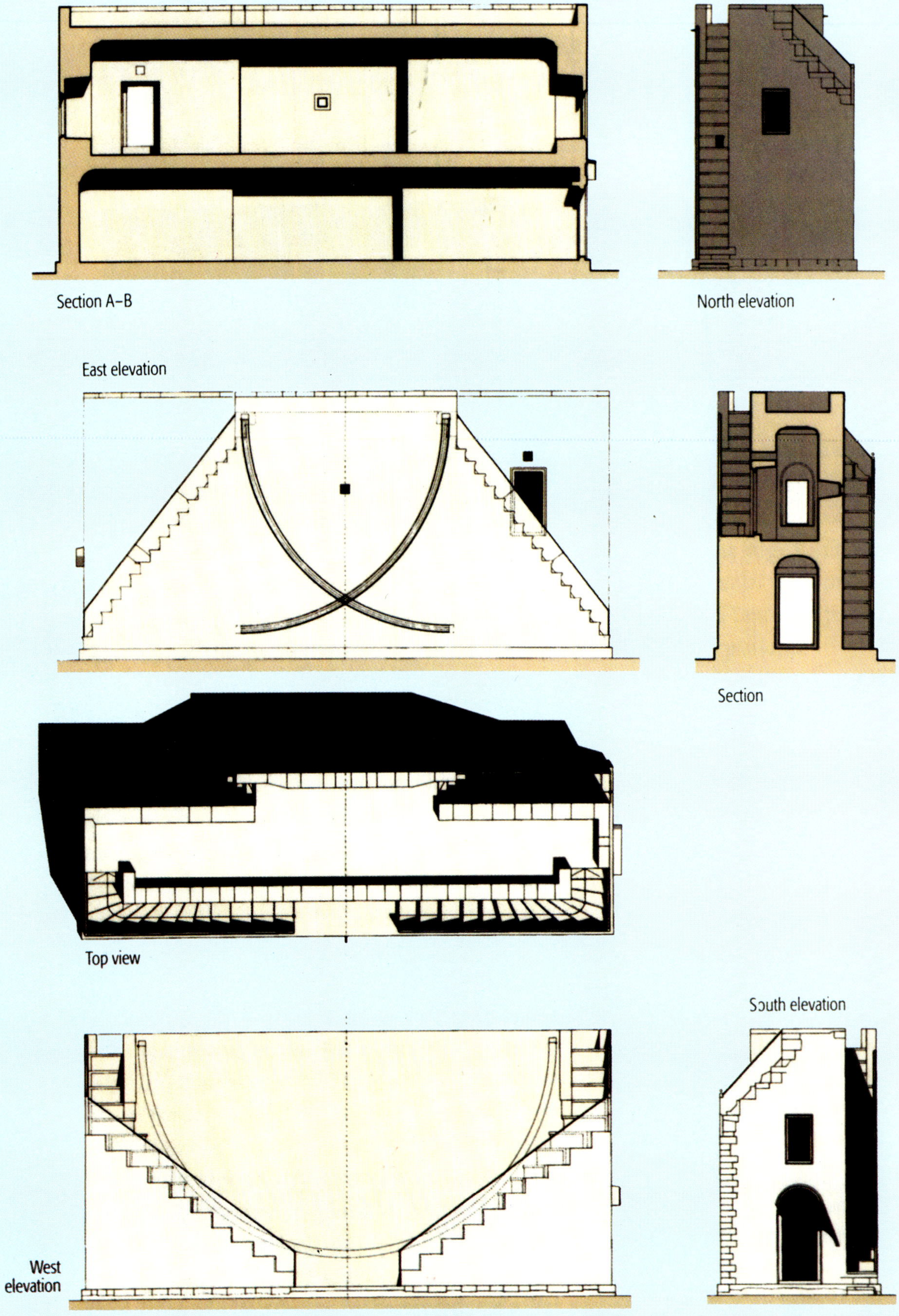

The Dakshinovritti Bhitti Yantra

Dakshinovritti Bhitti Yantra

It is also known as Meridinal-Wall Instrument. The Dakshinovritti Bhitti Yantra is situated in the north-eastern corner of this observatory. It is a vertical instrument built in the plane of the local meridian. The east face of the instrument is inscribed with two quadrants of 20 feet radius and on the west face a semi-circle of 19 feet 10 inches radius. These arcs are mainly constructed of white marble and graduated in degree as well as minutes. At the centres of quadrants and semi-circle, short pegs are fixed. The eastern and western faces of this instrument comprise two meridional instruments of slightly different shapes but meant for the same observations. The instr- ument is mainly used for observing the different altitudes of the heavenly bodies and Declination of the Sun.

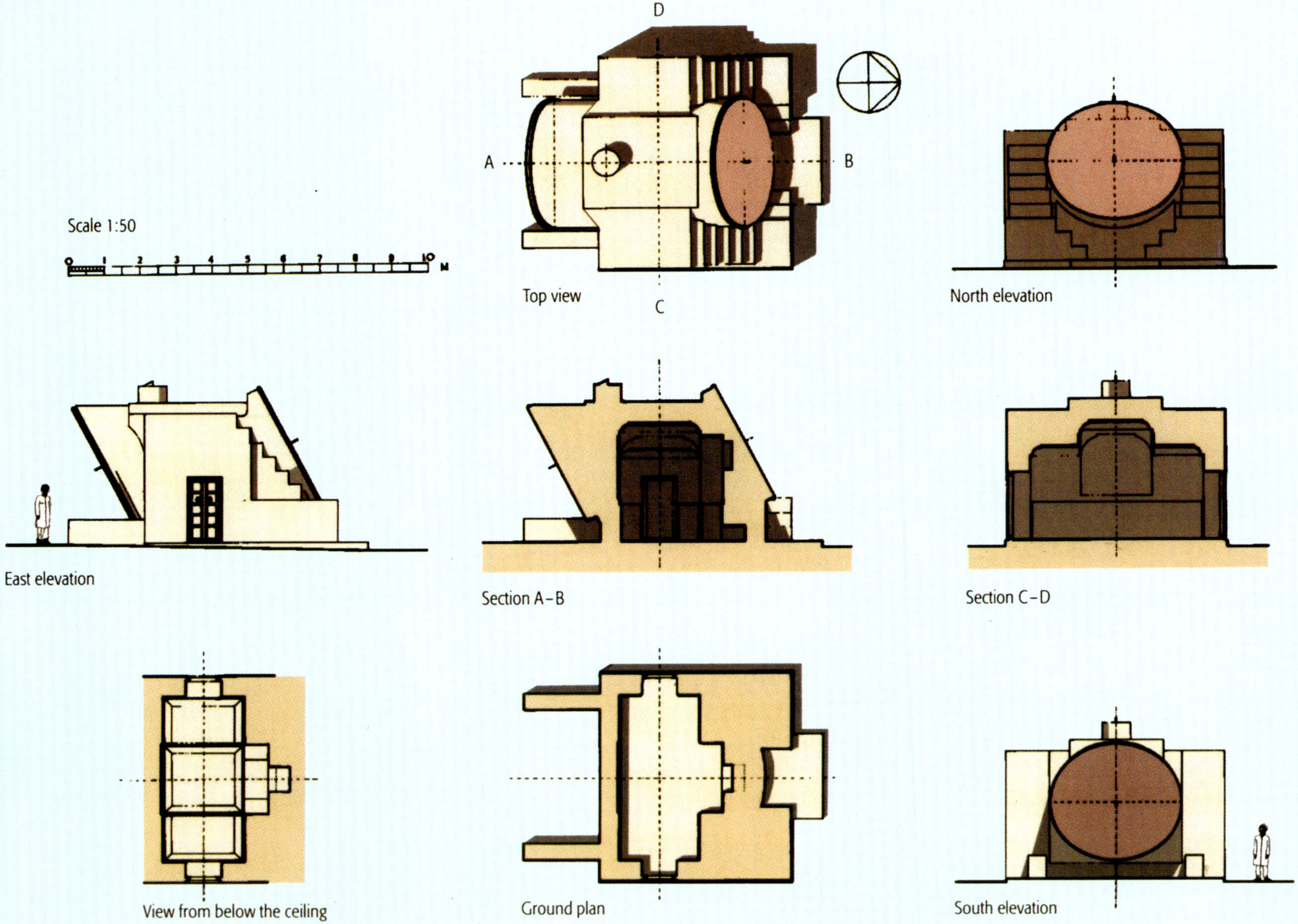

The Narivalaya Yantra

Narivalaya Yantra

This is an equatorial sundial of a different design from the Laghu Samrat Yantra, but performing the same function, it measures the local solar time at the latitude of Jaipur. There are only two paired instruments, one for use in winter between 23rd September-21st March (when the sun is in the southern hemisphere) and the other for use in summer between 21st march -23rd September, (when the sun is in the northern hemisphere). The instrument consists of a thin, rod-like gnomon fixed perpendicular to the masonry dial. The dial is set in the plane of the equator, and the gnomon points to the south pole (for the winter instrument) or the north pole (for the summer instrument. The inner portions of the dial is graduated in Ghatikas and palas, but the circumference is the same as hour and minute. Local solar time is read off from the angular position of the gnomon's shadow on the dial. Narivalaya Yantra helps in finding out the positions of Sun.

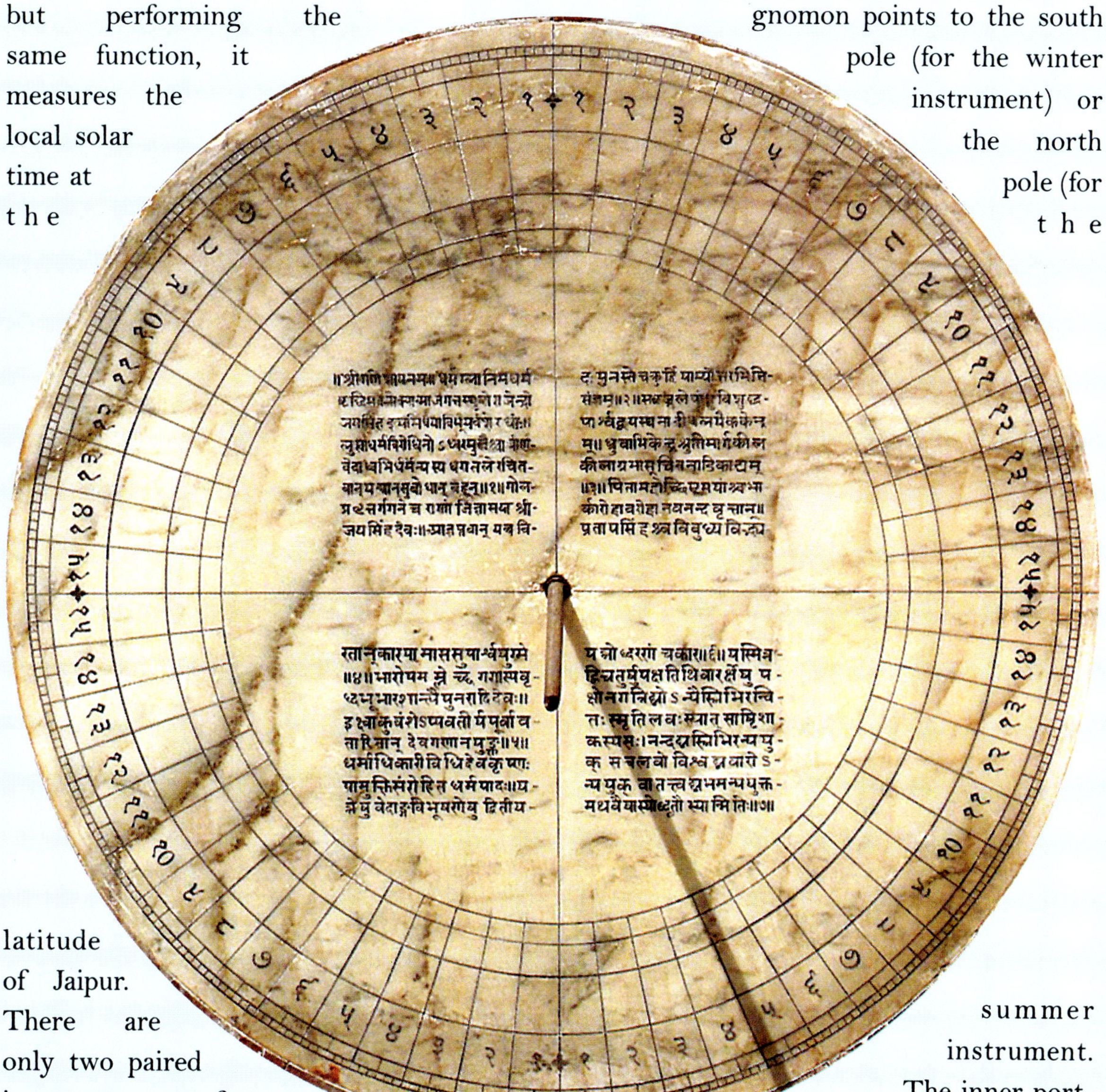

Krantivritta Yantra

It is also known as Ecliptic Instrument. It is situated north of the Northern Sun-Dial and is one of the few metal instruments of the Jaipur Observatory. It rotates on a masonry base, the stone circle is graduated in 60 ghatikas and the metal frame is graduated in 360 degrees. A separate metal tube is fixed in the hole at the centre of the metal frame for measuring celestial latitude and longitude. This instrument can be used at any time of day or night.

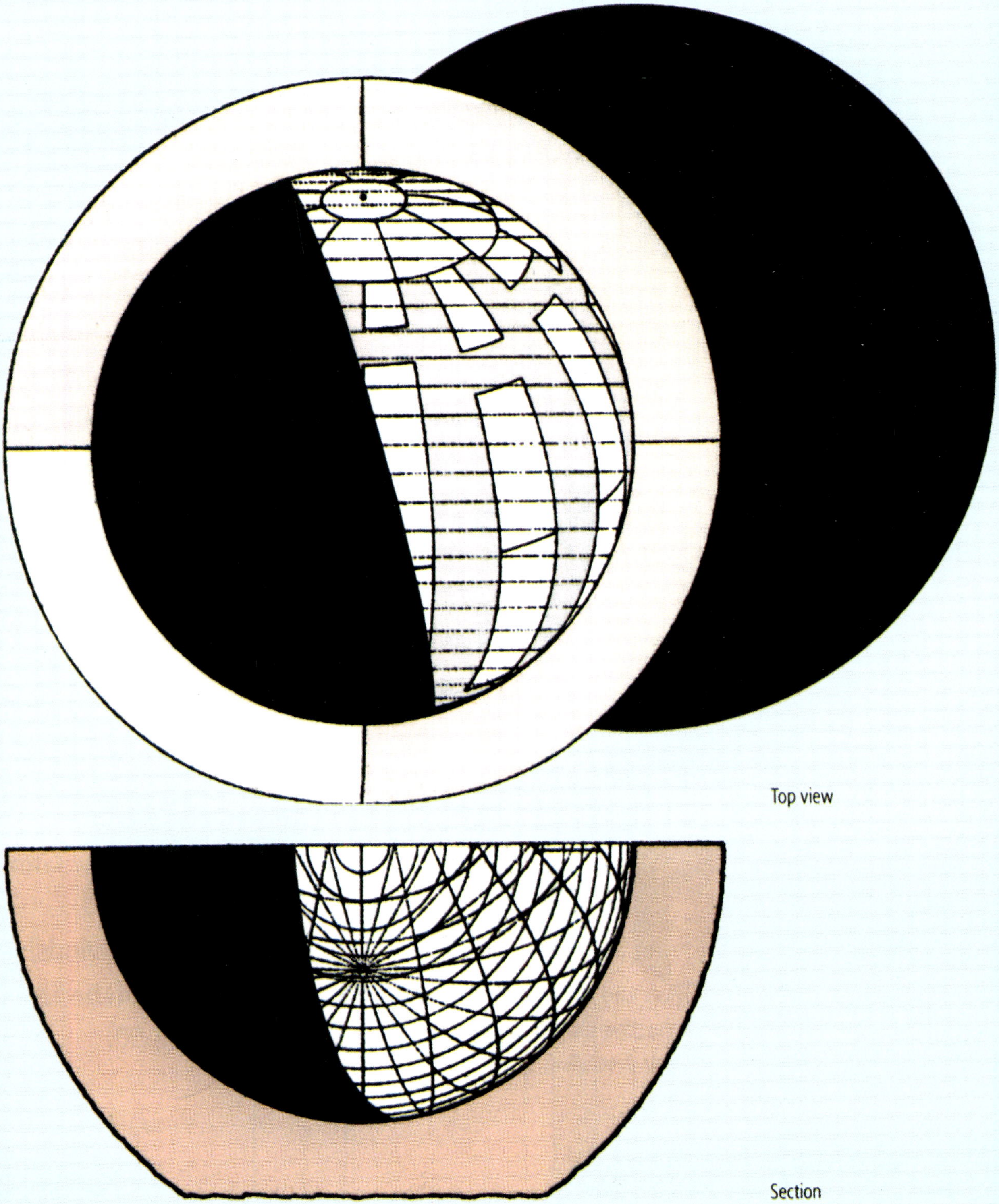

The Jai Prakash Yantra

Jai Prakash Yantra

Invented by Maharaja Sawai Jai Singh, this kaleidoscopic structure is known as 'Jai Prakash Yantra' - literally meaning the Light of Jai. It was built last and with the help of this instrument, the readings and calculations of other instruments could be verified and rectified.

It consists of two concave hemispherical marble bowls about 5.5 metres in diameter and represent the celestial hemispheres turned upside down. These two cavities are divided into six marble slabs, each one dividing further into minutes and seconds. They also bear inscriptions of 12 symbols of Zodiac. In the middle of the instrument hangs a ring which is representative of the sun. The marble slabs are divided in meridian and equator while the rim of the bowls represent the horizon which is graduated in 360 degrees.

The shadow of sun falls through the metal ring on the graduated surface . With the help of this, we are able to calculate Local time, Altitude, Azimuth, Meridian Pass time, Zenith Distance and Declination of the sun as well as its longitude.

This instrument can also be used for celestial observations during night for which the observer has to go inside the cavity and sit between the slabs. The celestial body is then observed through the hole of the metal ring.

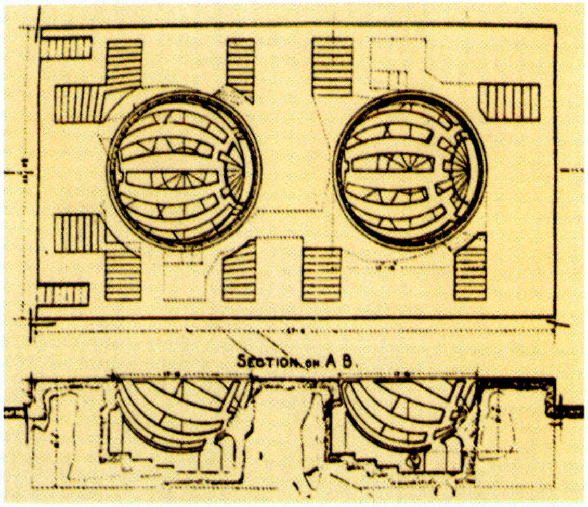

Yantra Raj

It is also known as the Great Astrolabe. Yantra Raj Karika is one of the proud possessions of the City Palace Museum, Jaipur. It is one of the largest astrolabes of the world. This astrolabe is almost 3 meter tall 2-12 meter across and 400 kg weight. This vertically hanging instrument is virtually a celestial map, neatly engraved on a huge seven-alloy metal disc of over 2 meter diameter. The hole at its centre is the Pole Star. Twenty-Seven degrees below this point, a prominent line represents the Local Horizon. The outermost circle is graduated in 60 'ghatikas' (equivalent to 24 hours) of 6 fractions each. The inner circle bears 360 degree markings, each of 6 sub-divisions. The northern most point of the local meridian line in this cob-web of circles, is the Zenith of Jaipur.

The positions of various constellations at different intervals can be calculated by placing a separate disc in the hole at the centre. A number of other astrological calculations such as the speed of rotation of the particular planet, dates of Sun and Moon eclipses as well as Sunset, Sunrise, Moon set etc. can also be calculated by using this "King of Instruments".

The Rashivalaya Yantra

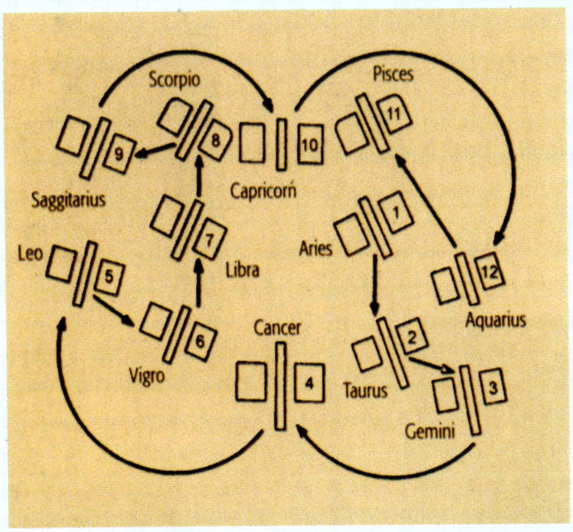

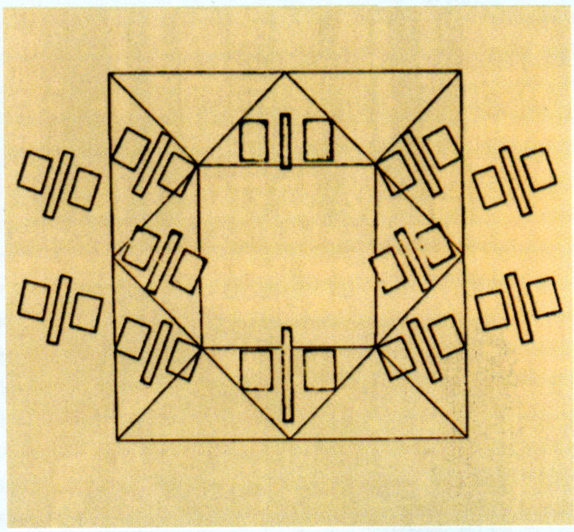

Rashivalaya Yantra

Known as 'Rashi Yantras' or the 'Rashivalaya', it is a group of 12 instruments representing all the 12 Zodiac Signs, situated on a rectangular platform near the southern wall of the observatory.

They look like smaller versions of the Equatorial Sun-Dial, but are quite different technically. The Quadrants of Samrat Yantra represents the equator while the quadrants of Rashivalaya represents the ecliptic at the moment of observation. The pole of the ecliptic is not a fixed point but is defined as a circle of 230 27' radius around the pole.

The angles of the gnomon of all the instruments are different from one another because each Zodiac sign is situated at a different position from the Ecliptic.

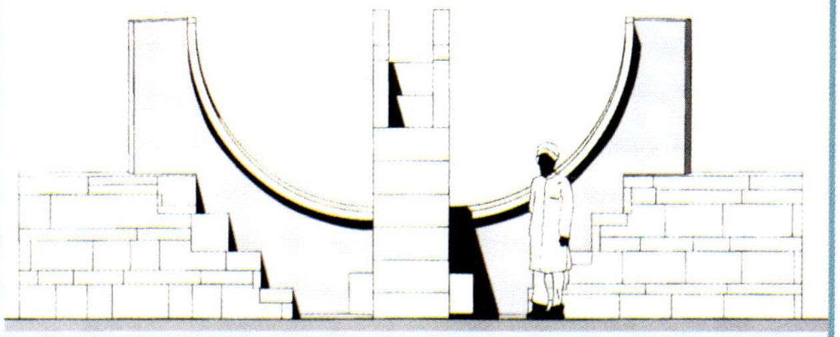

The instruments are used for observing latitudes and longitudes of the sun and the planets. Each instruments can be used every two hours when each sign of Zodiac reaches the local meridian. For calculating a particular sign of Zodiac culminating on the local meridian at the time of calculation, the Jai Prakash Yantra is used. For finding out the celestial position of the heavenly body, the corresponding zodiac instrument is used.

ZODIAC SIGNS

ZODIAC SIGNS	PERIODS	LUCKY CHARM	LUCKY COLOURS	LUCKY DAY
 Aries	21 March to 19 April	Diamond, Jasper, Blood Stone	Red, Crimson, Scarlet	Tuesday
 Taurus	20 April to 20 May	Sapphire, Diamond Amber, Coral, Emerald	Blue, Sea Green	Friday
 Gemini	21 May to 20 Junc	Emerald Pearl, Agate	Yellow	Saturday
 Cancer	21 June to 22 July	Emerald, Agate, Chalcedony Pearl, Ruby	Cream, Green	Monday
 Leo	23 July to 22 August	Peridot, Onyx, Amber Onyx	Gold, Orange	Sunday
 Virgo	23 August to 22 September	Carnelian, Sardonyx Jade, Sapphire	Grey	Wednesday
 Libra	23 September to 22 October	Opal, Chrysolite, Sardonyx Peridot	Pastel, Blue, Green	Friday
 Scorpio	23 October to 21 November	Aquamarine, Beryl	Dark Red, Crimson	Tuesday
 Sagittarius	22 November to 21 December	Topaz, Pearl Turquoise, Topaz	Purple, Lilac	Thursday
 Capricorn	22 December to 19 January	Ruby Garnet	Dark Green, Black, Grey	Saturday
 Aquarius	20 January to 18 February	Garnet, Hyacinth Opal, Amethyst	Pastel Shades of Blue, Green	Wednesday
 Pisces	19 February to 20 March	Amethyst Sapphire, Amethyst Bloodstone	Violet, Mauve, Lavender	Friday

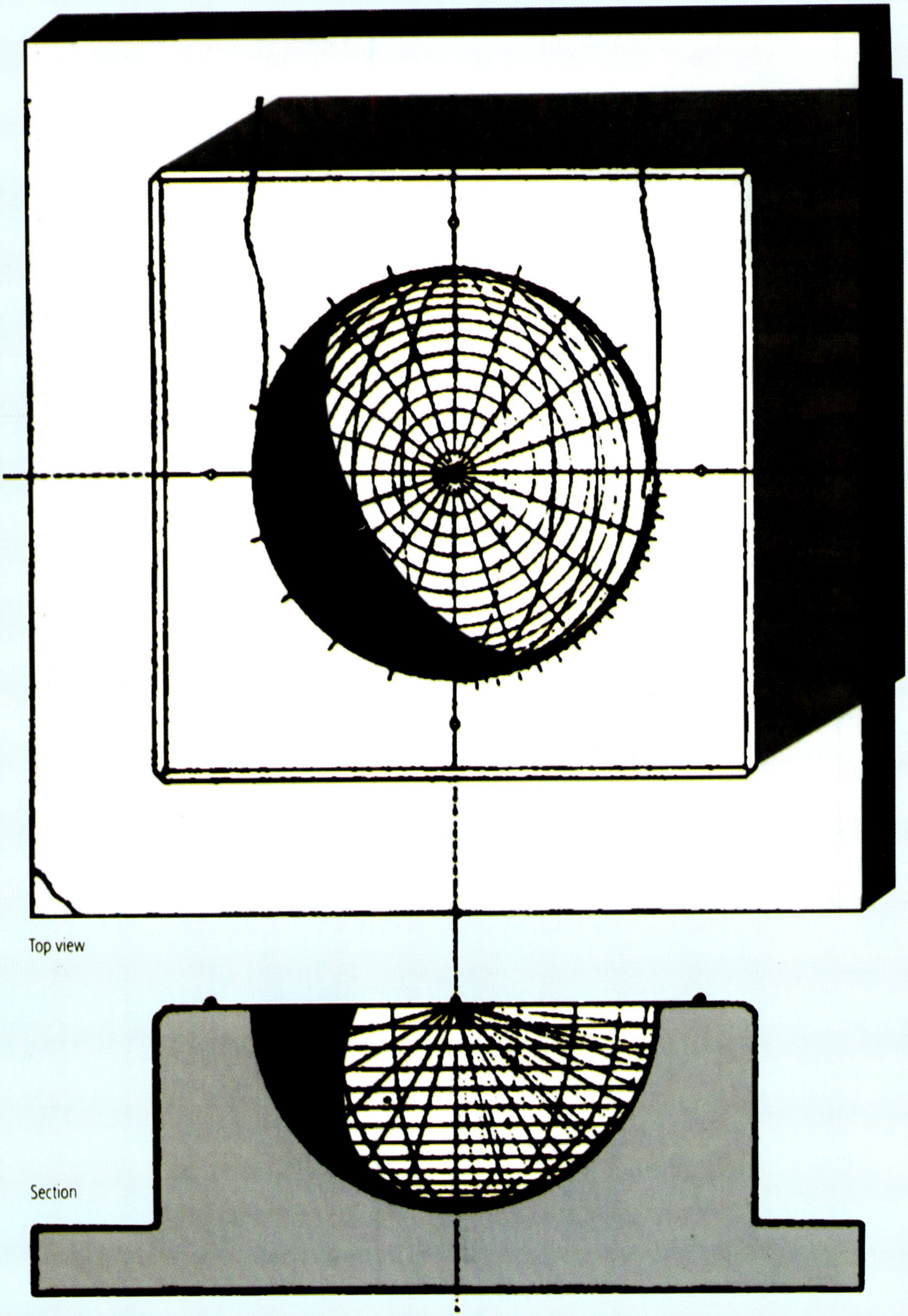

The Kapali Yantra

Kapali Yantra

These instruments are known as 'Kapali Yantras' which are located on a masonry platform in the western half of the observatory. They are two bowl shaped marble structures located on a masonry

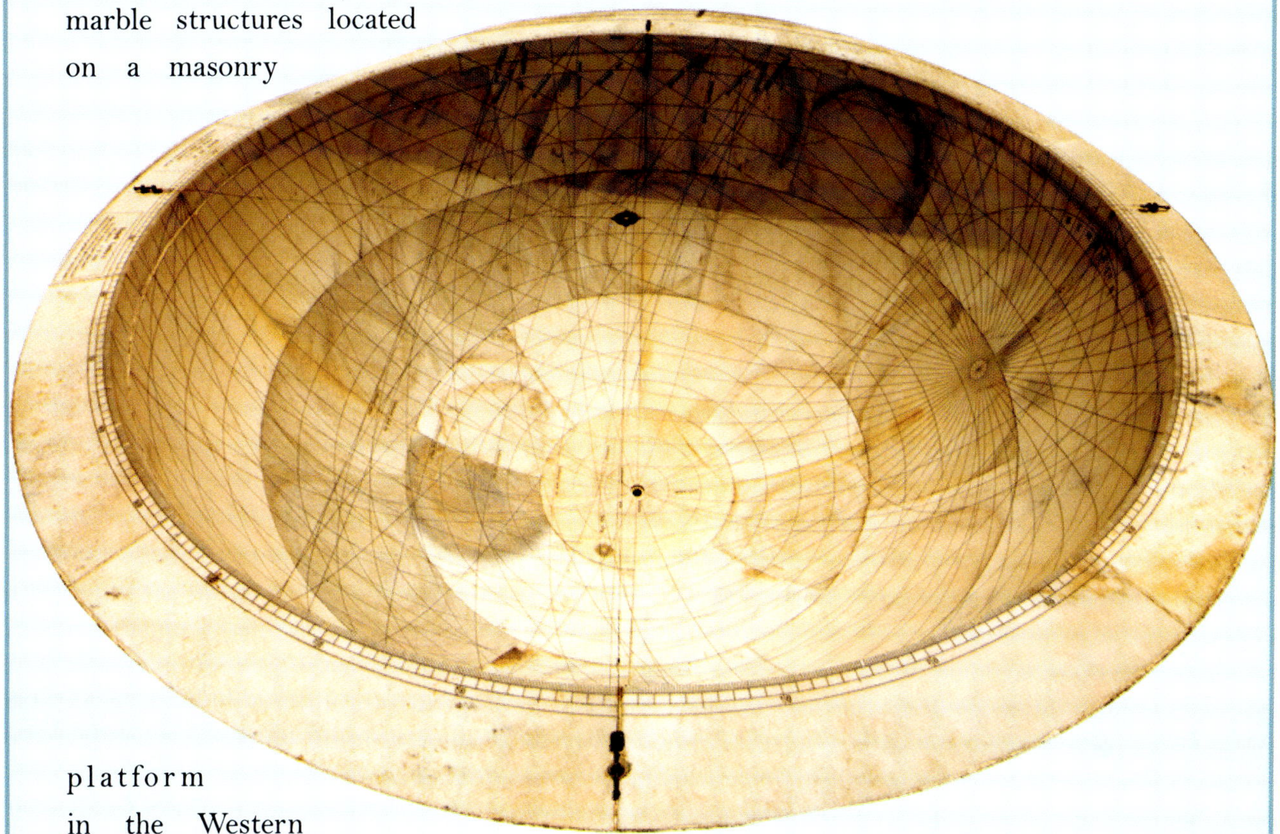

platform in the Western half of the observatory. Their horizons are calibrated from 0 degree to 90 degree and 90 degree to 180 degree and names of the twelve Zodiac sign are inscribed.

Eastern Kapali Yantra has various lines drawn criss-crossing its entire surface. It is not used for any observation but for solving astronomical problems graphically. Western Kapali Yantra is used to find out the Azimuth, Altitude, Meridian Pass Time, declination of Sun, local time etc., with the help of the shadow of the circular ring and on the graduations of the Kapali.

3

Chakra Yantra

There are two identical 'Chakra Yantras' framed on stone pillars located between the Eastern and Western Kapali Yantras. Made of an alloy of seven metals, each Yantra consists of a metal circle bearing 360 degree graduations. The metal bar is parallel to the celestial equator (27 degree angle) and has a hole at its centre where a brass tube is attached at the time of celestial observations.

The metal circles are free to move on their masonry, stand about a diameter parallel to the celestial equator. A metal disc is fitted near the southern axis of each 'Chakra Yantra' bearing the meridian line and 60 'ghatika' markings (equivalent to 24 hours).

A pointer is fixed in the hole provided in the southern axis of the Chakra, which moves on the graduated metal disc at the time of observation.

The sun or a planet is observed through the brass tube whose both extreme ends touch and move on the graduated circle.

The coinciding reading on the circle represents the declination of this particular object, and the position on the southern disc will be indicating Meridian Pass Time.

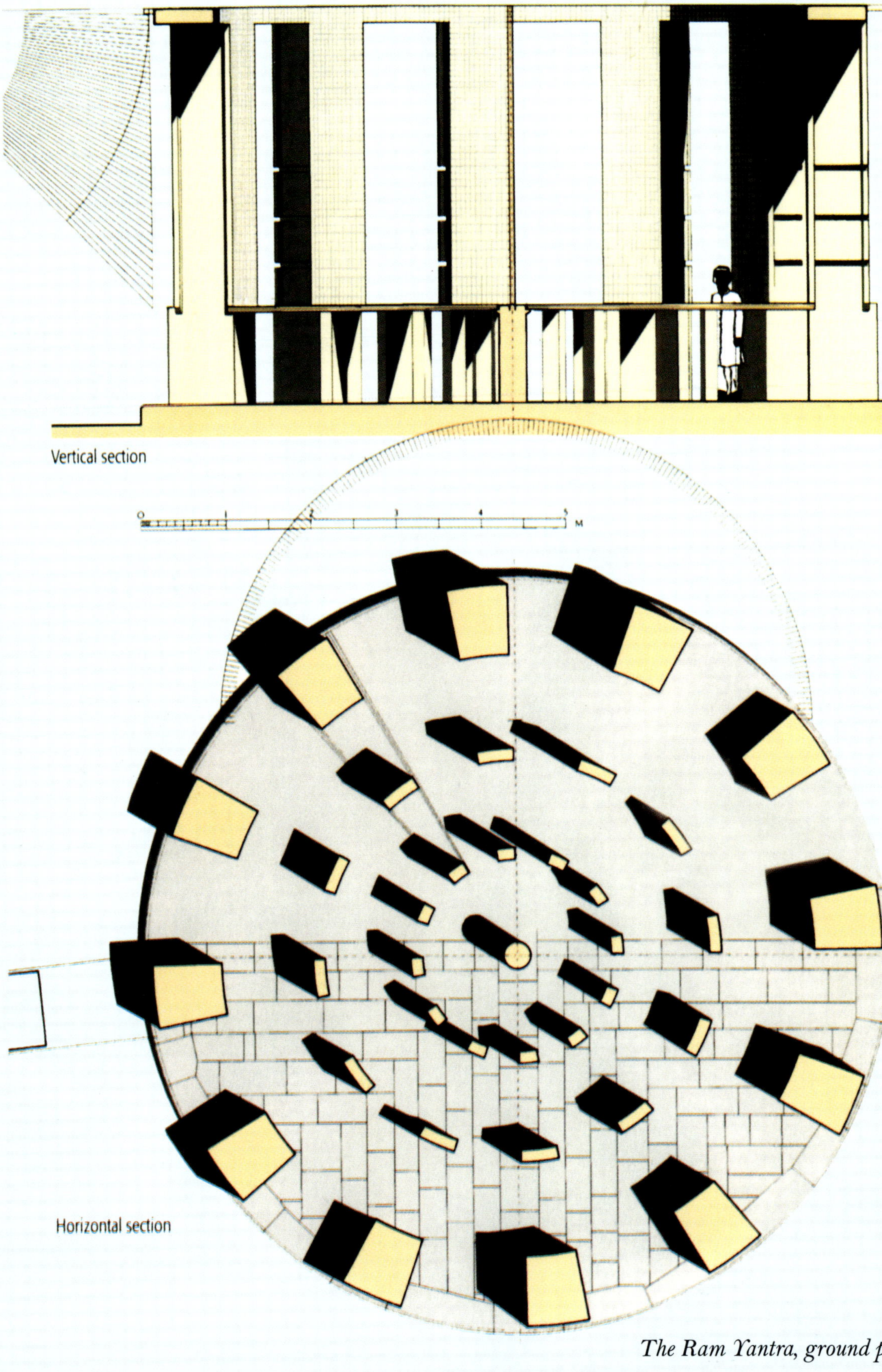

The Ram Yantra, ground plan

Vertical section

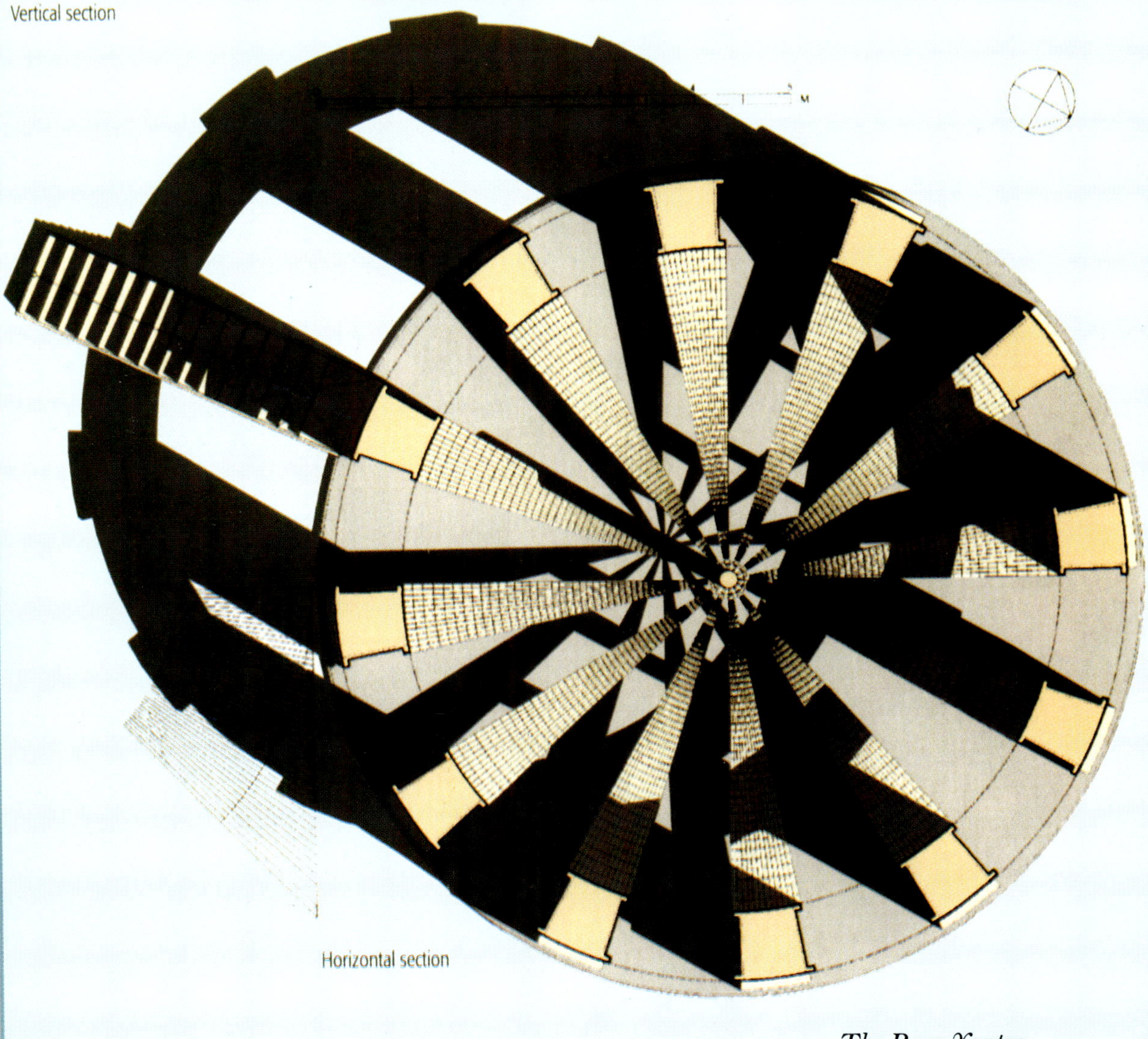

Horizontal section

The Ram Yantra,
vertical & horizontal section

Ram Yantra

Named after Maharaja Ram Singh, these two massive cylindrical structure are mainly used for calculating the Altitude and the Azimuth of the celestial bodies. They look identical and are used for similar observations, though at alternate time. These instruments give direct readings.

Consisting of twelve vertical columns and an equal number of horizontal slabs, the Ram Yantras represent the celestial sphere in inverted form; horizon on the top and zenith at the bottom of a centrally situated metal post. There are 360 vertical lines representing the azimuth circles and 90 horizontal lines or altitude circles. Each degree is subdivided by ten for the decimal calculations of azimuth and altitude of celestial objects during day and night.

During day time, we can read the celestial positions by observing the shadow of the central rod. During night, the observer has to go inside the instrument and watch the object through the top of the central rod. This is also an instrument by which we come to know the movement of stars, and thus the weather forecasts.

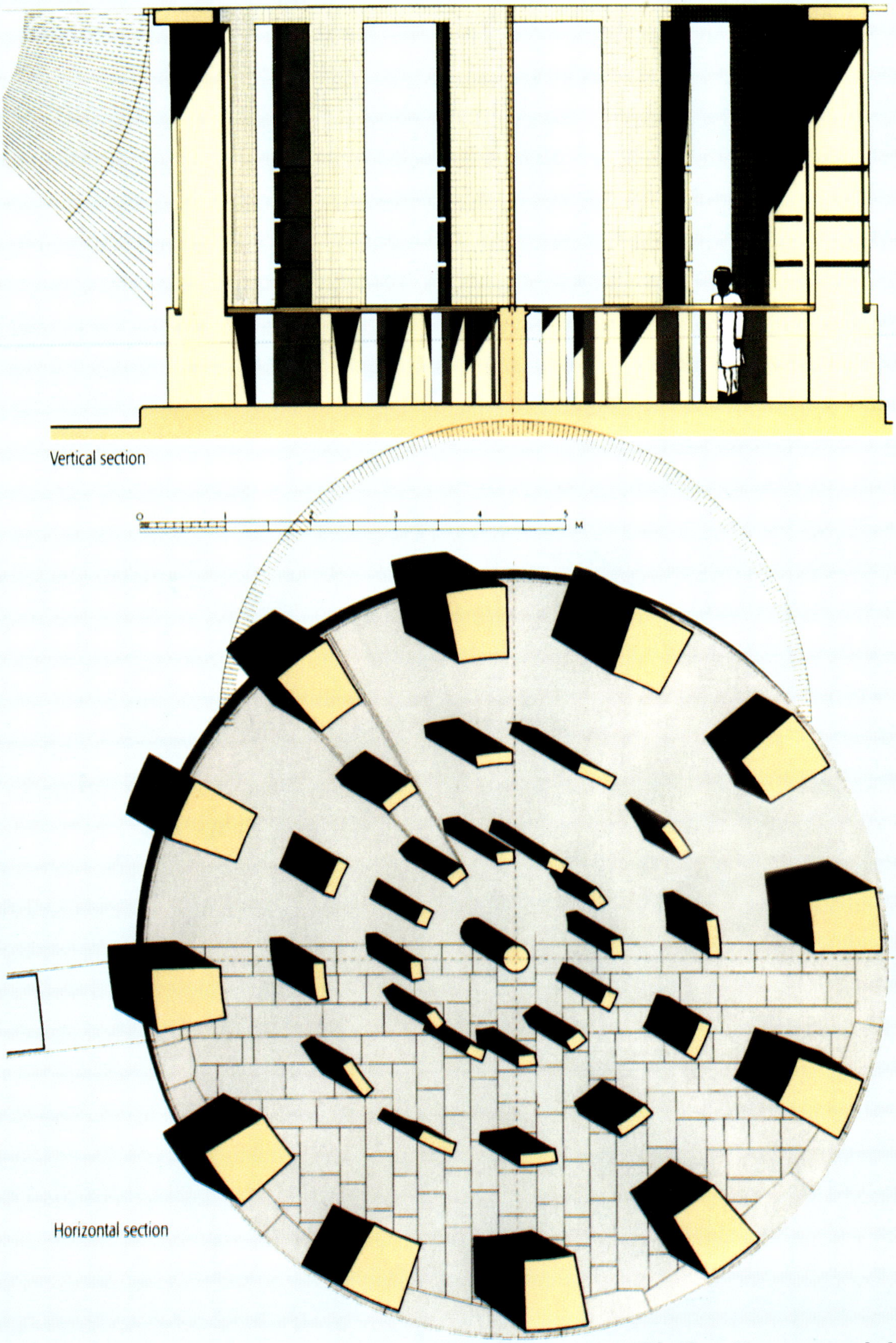

The Ram Yantra, ground plan

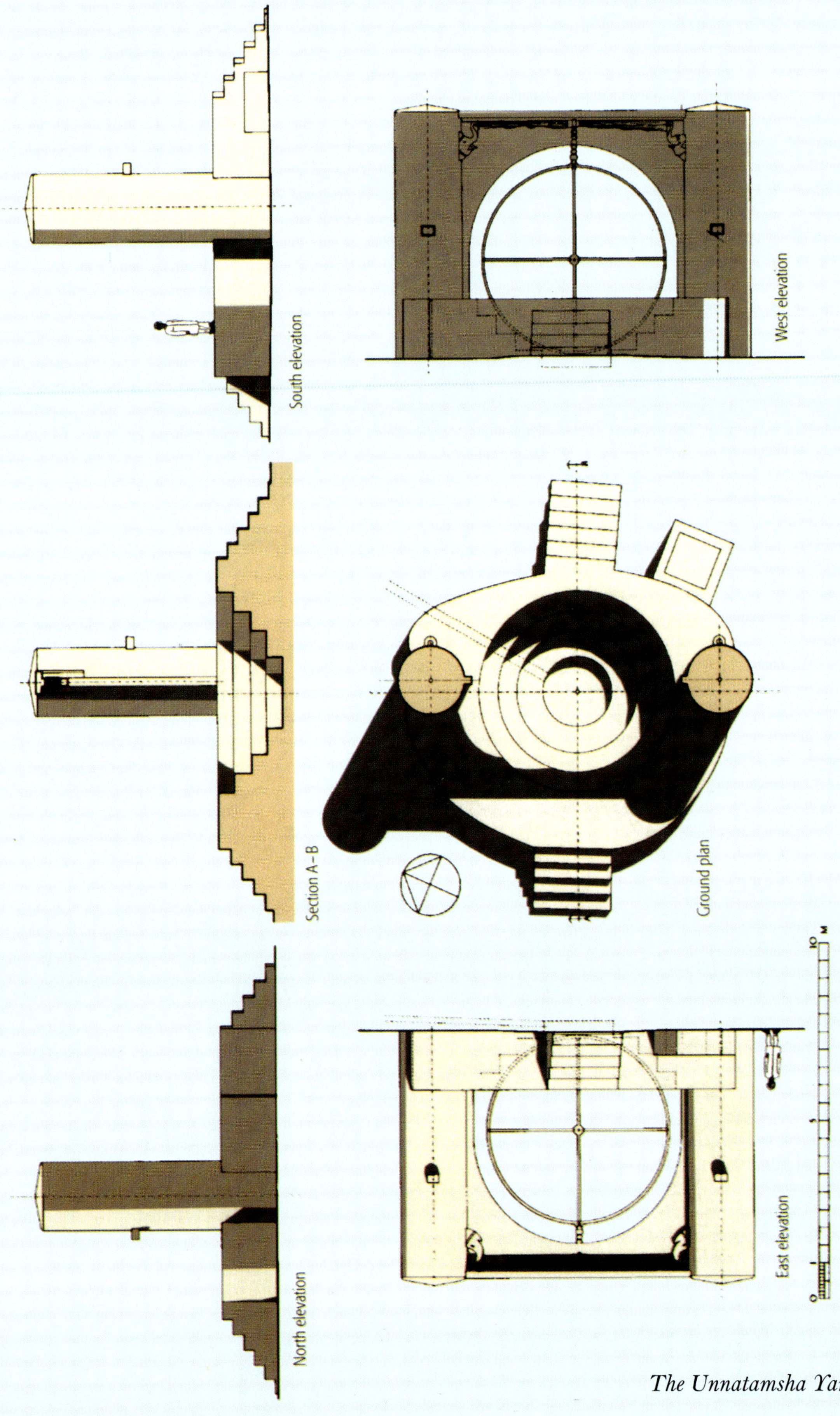

The Unnatamsha Yantra

Unnatamsha Yantra

The 'Unnatansha Yantra' is another important metal instrument which is situated in the north-eastern corner of this observatory.

It is a big metal circle of about five metre diameter hanging in vertical plane on a massive masonry support. The suspension of this heavy metal circle in a hollow space below, allows it to rotate in the vertical plane for the purpose of celestial observations. The entire cirlce of 4 equal segments of 90 degrees each, is thus, graduated in 360 degrees, each of 10 parts. There is a hole at the centre of the Altitude Instrument where a pointer is fixed at the time of observation.

The 'Yantra' is used to determine the celestial altitude of heavenly bodies, at any time during day or night.

Digamsha Yantra

Known as 'Digamsha Yantra', the Azimuth Instrument is situated north of both the Ram Yantras and west of the Kapali Yantra. It consists of three circular constructions, one inside the other, made in the plane of horizon. There is a massive round structure of about 1 metre height at the centre which is encircled by a circular wall of the same height and of about 5 metre diameter. The outermost masonry circle of about 2 metre height, is made of 8 metre diameter. All the three masonry structures have marble tops precisely graduated in 360 degrees each as they represent the horizon circles. The degrees are further subdivided in decimals. Two metal wires are tightly stretched across the outermost circle and they represent the North-South and East-West directions respectively. At the centre, supported by these wires is a metal knob.

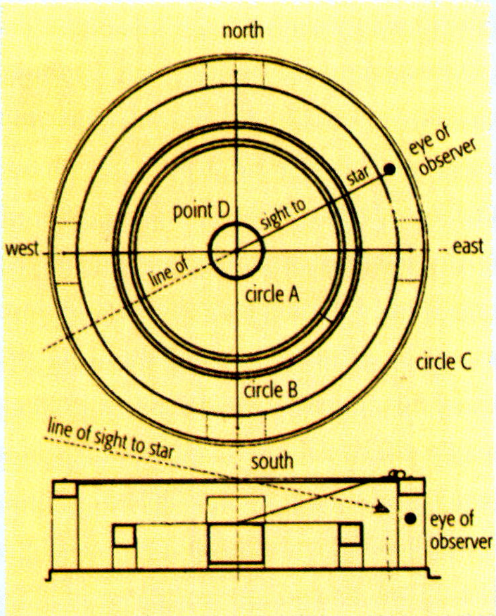

This is the most accurate instrument for determining the Azimuth of the sun. This is done by observing the shadow of the ring on the floor. Then a thread is tied to the knob and taken to the outermost wall passing through the shadow of the ring. The reading of the horizon on the third wall is the Azimuth of Sun. Further, sun's rising and setting time can also be calculated by this instrument.

Glossary

Astronomy	The science of observation and determination of motions, distances and positions of the heavenly bodies in the celestial sphere.
Stars	Fixed large globes of intensely heated gas. They shine by their own light. The Sun is a star.
Planets	Large spherical bodies which revolve round the Sun in elliptical orbits. Mercury, Venus, mars, Jupiter, Saturn, Uranus, Neptune and Pluto are planets. The Earth is also a planet.
Celestial Equator	A great circle, drawn east to west, divides the celestial sphere into two equal parts, known as Northern and Southern Hemispheres. The Sun comes on the celestial equator on the 21st March and 23rd September, making equal duration of day and night known as Vernal Equinox and Autumnal Equinox respectively.
Tropics	Capricorn is South. Between the two tropics lies the torrid zone.
Local Celestial Meridian	The great circle is drawn North-South through the Zenith. The Sun comes on this imaginary line at local (mid-day) 12 O'Clock every day.
Zenith	It is the highest point in the celestial sphere above the observer. The Zenith distance of celestial objects is measured in relation to this point.
Nadir	The point where a vertical line extended directly below the observer meets the celestial sphere on the other side of the earth.
Declination	It is the angular distance of a heavenly object North or South of the celestial equator.
Altitude	It is the distance of a heavenly body vertically above the horizon. It is measured through 90 degrees.
Azimuth	It is the horizontal angle between a heavenly body and the South point of the horizon. It is measured westward through 360 degrees in horizontal plane or from the north point eastward.

Glossary

Celestial Latitude	It is the angular distance of a heavenly body measured from zero degree to 90 degrees North or South of the celestial equator. The geographic latitude parallels are drawn on the globe, at a distance of about 111 kms. from each other.
Celestial Longitude	A co-ordinate in the ecliptic system, it is the angular distance of a heavenly body from the vernal equinox along the ecliptic towards east measured from zero degree to 360 degrees.
Geographic Longitude	A co-ordinate system on the surface of the earth, the angle between the meridian passing thorough a position and the Prime Meridian (Green which) measured east or west from zero degree to 180 Degrees.
Ecliptic	It is a great imaginary circle, representing the apparent annual orbit of the Sun up to the celestial sphere, caused by the actual revolution of the earth around the Sun.
Equinoxes	These are two points where the great circle of the ecliptic intersects the great circle of the celestials equator. This happens twice a year, on the 21st March and 23rd September known as Vernal Equinox and Autumnal Equinox respectively, causing equal duration of day and night.
Meridian	It is an angle of 23 degrees 26 minutes 54 seconds made by the intersection of the ecliptic and equator circles.
Zodiac Signs	A series of twelve constellations along the ecliptic circle named (with the exception of Libra) after living creatures.
Zodiac Circle	It is an eighteen degree wide belt around the ecliptic. It is divided into 12 Zodiac signs of 30 degrees each.
Right Ascension	It is the angular distance of a body measured along the equator in an easterly direction from a fixed point on the equator.
Declino-Meter	An instrument for measuring the declination of the compass i.e. the deviation of the magnetic needle from the true north.
Astrology	It is the study of the motions, and positions of the stars and planets and their influence on human life.